25 Things to Do

When Grandpa Passes Away,
Mom and Dad Get Divorced,
or the Dog Dies

Activities to Help Children Suffering Loss or Change

by Laurie A. Kanyer, MA, CFLE
illustrated by Jenny Williams

Parenting Press, Inc.
Seattle, Washington

Disclaimer
The information and activities in this book are not intended to substitute for other services to aid children in integrating the losses of their lives. This book is a basic primer on
grief and includes a sampling of activities that can help children reconcile and accept
their life circumstances. Providing grief counseling and grief support groups for children is
highly recommended.

Text and illustrations copyright © 2004 by Parenting Press, Inc.

Edited by Carolyn J. Threadgill
Designed by Margarite Hargrave Design
Printed in the United States of America

Library of Congress Cataloging-in-Publication Data

Kanyer, Laurie A., 1959-
    25 things to do when grandpa passes away, mom and dad get divorced, or the dog dies :
activities to help children suffering loss or change / Laurie A. Kanyer ; illustrated by
Jenny Williams.
        p. cm.
    Includes index.
    ISBN 1-884734-54-5 -- ISBN 1-884734-53-7 (pbk.)
    1. Grief in children. 2. Loss (Psychology) in children. 3. Children–Counseling of.
I. Title: Twenty five things to do when grandpa passes away, mom and dad get divorced,
or the dog dies. II. Title.

    BF723.G75K36 2004
    155.9'37'083–dc21

                                                                        2003048264

Parenting Press, Inc.
P.O. Box 75267, Seattle, WA 98175
Telephone (206) 364-2900
www.ParentingPress.com

Dedication

To my daughters Elisabeth and Kirsten, who sustained the deaths of two close friends in their childhood, and to my son Wyatt, who survived a life-threatening illness in his childhood.

To my sister Elisabeth Pedemonte and my brother Chris Valderhaug, who shared with me traumatic childhood losses due to death and divorce.

To my mother Lucy Valderhaug, who intuitively knew how to help us cope with our grief in artistic ways.

To my husband Doug Kanyer, the sturdiest, most centered person I know—my lighthouse!

Preface: How to Help Grieving Children

Since you are reading this book, you may be worried about a child who has suffered a significant loss. You also may be suffering a loss and be in great pain yourself. No matter what caused you to pick up this book, I doubt that you ever imagined yourself in the situation you are in now. Rarely can we anticipate or prepare for loss.

Death and other significant losses challenge every person who experiences them, adult and child alike. All aspects of our person are affected: physical, spiritual, emotional, social, and intellectual.

All children express grief similarly, through their behavior. The extent of their grief is based on the depth of involvement or importance the person or pet held for the child. Children in foster care or adopted, those who move a great deal or whose friends move away, or who suffer debilitating accidents or illness can also suffer tremendous feelings of grief. Other losses in a child's life can loom disproportionately large and produce grief, such as not being chosen for the team or not getting first place. Regardless of the circumstance of the loss or change, the activities in this book will help children who are grieving.

25 Things to Do . . . is a collection of simple, time-tested, down-to-earth activities to manage the emotional tone of childhood loss.

You will be able to help your child most effectively if you read Part One before selecting the activity you think will benefit your child.

I wish you and your children peace as you go about integrating loss into your lives.

Part One

What You Need to Know About Grief

Basic (and Important) Information About Grief

Grieving is the experience we all go through to understand loss in our lives. We do not "get over" loss; grieving is a life-long process. As children grow, their grief is recycled over their lifetime. At each new developmental stage, they will probably think about the loss and wonder what their lives would have been like if it hadn't happened.

The purpose of grieving is to incorporate loss into our life stories. Getting used to and accepting loss are the goals of grief work. You, as a caring adult, can offer activities that will help children accept loss and live with it.

Grief is experienced and expressed physically

When anyone experiences the death of a loved one or a beloved pet or the loss of a parent in the home due to divorce, their grief is expressed as emotional energy released into the body. This energy shoots through the body, flooding every cell with physical impulses and memories. The brain and body are strongly linked during such times of emotional upheaval. A child's entire system operates in a cooperative reaction, alerting all parts of his or her person to the change.

Grief has no time table

Time feels suspended during grief, as if it didn't exist. When we grieve, our days may seem to run together, appearing to have no beginning and no end, or have big gaps, when we cannot remember what happened or what we did. Grief also fits no predetermined time line. It cannot be hurried. Each person grieves at his or her own pace.

How Grieving Children Feel

Each child experiences grief in a unique way

Each child will express his or her loss in an individual style. You need to know that no two children in your family will grieve in the same manner; each child's way of coping will be unique to him or her.

Children's developmental stage affects their understanding of death

There is a wide range of understanding of death in children based on their ages. A two-year-old, for example, will not be able to understand that a dead person is not alive and will not come back to life. A five-year-old can understand that death is not reversible, it is final. A seven-year-old may have a need to understand the mechanics of the cause of death and may want information about exactly what happened. A twelve-year-old is developmentally capable of formulating ideas and beliefs and questions about an afterlife.

The deeper your child's felt connection to the person or pet, the deeper your child's pain

The depth of grief experienced by a child will be based upon how close the child felt to someone who has died or moved away. Children have their own interpretations of their relationships to others. Even within the same family, individual children will behave differently after a loss based upon how each perceived his or her relationship with the missing person or pet.

Grief is confusing

Grief can be a very confusing and scary experience for children. Because of the grief energy flooding their bodies, children can feel bewildered, even forgetful. They may experience a range of emotions and behavior that may be new to them, that they have not felt before, such as aggression, withdrawal, guilt, clinging, tantrums, and moodiness.

Many of these feelings happen all at once—children can be both angry and excited at the same time. New fears and worries may come up as they wonder what will happen to them, or if someone else may die or leave. They may worry about their safety and who will take care of them.

Grief has a cumulative effect

Each child has his or her own personal grief history based on how much loss has occurred in his or her life. Each new loss builds upon prior losses in a child's life.

Grieving children experience an altered state of awareness

During times of loss, children function from an altered state of awareness. It's as if they see themselves as characters in a make-believe story. Their brains and bodies are working so hard to come to terms with the loss that they literally feel suspended in some other kind of living. Consequently, grieving children sometimes cannot talk about the event.

Children need to be told they are not responsible

When major life loss occurs, such as death or divorce, children often blame themselves. They may feel they caused the death or divorce and if they had acted differently, it would not have happened. This misconception needs to be cleared up as quickly as possible. Children deserve to know that they did nothing to make a person die or their parents get divorced.

Tasks and emotions of grieving children

There are three major tasks and a number of emotions children experience while grieving, as follows:

- **Understanding** that the person or pet is dead or has moved away permanently. The degree to which a child understands death or divorce is determined by the child's developmental stage and how old the child is when the person dies or moves away.
- **Experiencing** emotions that wind in and out during grieving, not in any particular order, including:

    Shock, which is dependent upon the nature of the death or other loss. Shock is more severe if the loss was sudden and unanticipated.

    Denial, an unwillingness to accept that the person or pet has died or left.

    Guilt, a lack of understanding that there was nothing the child could do to prevent the loss.

    Anger, ranging from strong protest and aggression to rebellion.

    Fear, a worry over who might die next, who would care for the child, and whether or not the child himself might die soon.

    Sorrow, a loss of security and utter helplessness as to how one lives without the person who died or left.

Bargaining, an attempt to make a trade for the return of the person or pet that died.

Acceptance, beginning to accept life as it is now after the loss. (This does not mean getting over it because grief is recycled over a lifetime.)

- **Building** new relationships while still remembering the person or pet who has died or is gone.

How Grieving Children Behave

Children need physical activities to help them cope

Children act out grief in physical ways because they may not yet be able developmentally to express themselves verbally as most adults do. They may need to play act, or make believe, what has happened and to release grief energy through small and large muscle activities.

When children have opportunities to do activities such as those presented here, their grief energy can be released. They can transform the grief energy into resolution and acceptance.

Crying helps

Crying is a natural way to release grief energy. Certain chemicals in the body that help children feel better are released when they cry. Crying may help some children enough to begin to express their thoughts and feelings, too. This is what you need to know about crying:

- Crying can come and go without warning, at unexpected (and sometimes inconvenient) times.
- Children may cry over simple frustrations that never bothered them before, like dropping a toy, a shoe that won't stay tied, or food not fixed exactly as they wished.
- Children will feel more comfortable about crying if they see adults cry, too. Do not try to hide your tears.
- Crying is healthy; it is not a sign of weakness. It indicates that you recognize your loss and are beginning to accept it. It is also an appropriate expression of sadness.

Behavior that looks like aggression and withdrawal is typical

As children grieve, they experience random memories and impulses of emotion physically. Any range of behavior can occur. Some children may act angry, aggressive, or withdrawn. Children may not talk as much, they may rock back and forth, holding themselves. They need to know and be told that feeling angry is typical during grief.

Children need to know that they will not be allowed to hurt themselves or anyone else. Reassure them that you will help them with their angry feelings and keep them safe, and provide physical activities for them to express whatever they are feeling safely.

Temperament affects a child's expression of grief

Some children *appear* to feel grief more intensely than others due to their behavior. Highly intense or emotionally sensitive children will react in more obvious outward ways than children who have more moderate temperaments. But both groups feel grief and need the same kinds of support.

How to Help Grieving Children

Children need activities to help them cope with loss

In order to make sense of loss and to cope with the natural outpouring of grief energy, children need physical and tactile activities to manage their bodies' grief energy. Activities that use large muscles and small muscles assist in the release of grief energy.

Children need repetitive motions to cope with random memories and impulses of grief energy

Repetitive motions can help children cope with the flow of random grief energy. Whether pouring water or scooping sand, every opportunity for repeat motion is helpful.

Children need to act out their feelings

Children benefit by taking part in undirected play acting (like make believe). This process takes place in symbolic actions that have unique meaning to each individual child. By play acting scenes in their lives, children are better able to comprehend and accept how their lives have become reorganized or changed. Caring adults can learn to simply observe a child's symbolic play

acting and to reflect what they see the child doing, rather than trying to interpret it.

Children need to create visual memorials of remembrance

Making a Memory Book or a photo collage, a visual object that represents or honors the person or pet, can be very helpful for grieving children.

There is no expectation of a perfect end result in making a memorial. By exploring creative activities a child's capacity to reflect, recall, and remember is increased, while at the same time constructively expelling grief energy.

Grieving children need adults to be available and present

Remember, too, that there is value in being quietly present and available. This helps children understand that they are not alone.

Children understand themselves and their lives based on predictable interactions with others. They may feel like they don't exist when someone dies or leaves the family due to divorce. By being present with grieving children you become the mirror for their continued existence.

Talking About Death and Divorce

Spend extra time with children

Communication is more likely if you are available for your children. Make more time in your daily schedule for them. Conversations are more likely when there are more chances for them to occur.

Correct information is vital

Children have rich imaginations; they may imagine the worst case scenario regarding the loss. Take every opportunity you get to give them straightforward, accurate information. You will need to do this more than once or twice. Never assume children understand fully based upon a few conversations. They usually need to "build" their understanding of what has happened, to add layers like bricks in a wall.

Children need to know they are not to blame

Children often feel guilty, as if there were something they personally could have done—or not done—that would change the situation. They need your reassurance that they are not responsible. You might say, "Grandpa's heart was very sick. He had a heart attack and he died." Or, "Your mom and dad had difficulty getting along. They decided to get a divorce." Always add to any explanation, "I want you to know you did not cause this to happen. You are not responsible."

Use accurate words to describe what happened

Explaining death or divorce to children is not an easy task. Even so, do not use language that may be confusing to a child. Avoid such terms as "sleeping" to describe death, or "gone away for a while" to describe divorce. Instead, use words that have one meaning: dying, dead, death, divorce, separation. Children will begin to understand that the situation will not change when adults around them communicate clearly about the finality of the loss.

Children tend to generalize

If Grandpa died in the hospital, a child may assume that everyone who goes to the hospital will die. Or if the child is told Grandpa died "because he was sick," the child may decide everyone who gets sick will die. Reassure children that most illnesses and injuries improve on their own or with rest or medicine. A child may think that *any* married couple who has a disagreement or appears to be fighting (or is fighting) is going to get a divorce, if his or her parents did. Reassure children that most adults can disagree without it leading to divorce.

Be prepared for questions at awkward times

Sometimes children will ask an important question when it is an uncomfortable time for you to answer accurately and fully. Say, "I'm so glad you brought that up. I've been wanting to talk about that, too." Then say, "Since we're in the store, I'm distracted. Let's talk about that question as soon as we get to the car [or get home]." Be sure to remember to have the conversation so that your child knows it's okay to talk about loss.

Provide words for your child to use with other people

Someone, another child or an adult, will probably ask what happened. The question is likely to be an innocent one, such as, "I haven't seen your big black dog around lately. Do you still have her?" Your child will need to be able to answer honestly, if he or she wishes to answer at all.

Give your child words to describe what happened. Imagine how much more comfortable he or she will feel, being able to answer: "My dog died last month. I really miss her." Or, "My father died in a boating accident." Or, "My mom and dad are divorced. I see Mom every weekend." Or, "I really prefer not to talk about that right now."

Children need reassurance regarding their daily schedule during times of loss or change

During times of change children crave information that will help them feel safe and nurtured. For example, they might worry about who will take care of them, who will take them home from school, or who will prepare their meals.

Maintain a regular routine as much as possible. Tell your children what the routine will be. Write out what the new routine will be. If you have to change it, be prepared for your children to have an emotional response. This is normal!

Talking About Pets

The relationship a child has to his or her pet can be one of the strongest bonds of childhood. Pets offer predictable love and companionship. They listen without comment and love their owners unconditionally. Owning any kind of pet, from a goldfish to a horse, offers children a chance to give of themselves and to learn responsibility for another living being. Even if you felt no strong connection to the pet in your household, be aware that your child may have felt very strongly indeed.

A pet's death is often a child's first experience with loss through death. This experience can create a powerful blueprint for the way children learn to express grief. The death of a pet is also a good time for parents to help children learn about the cycle of life and death common to all living things. It is a good time to begin to help children recognize loss and change and learn skills to

cope with these recurring aspects of life. (Sometimes pets myste-
riously disappear or run away. Your child will need help coping
with this loss in the same manner as if it were a death.)

All the principles of childhood grief apply to the loss or death of
a pet. The way grief is expressed in childhood is the same, whether
the loss is of a person or an animal. Treat your child as tenderly at
this time as you would if it were Grandpa who had died.

Talking About Feelings

Just because children may not be talking about their losses doesn't
mean they are not thinking about them. They may be hesitant to
talk because they don't want to upset the adults around them.
Children learn how to behave by watching other people. Some
adults try to protect children by not sharing feelings or talking
about the loss. The most harmful signal adults give children is to
make death a secret by avoiding talking about it in front of them.
By expressing your feelings and speaking clearly, accurately, and
often, you help children express their own feelings.

Expand children's vocabulary

Children need adults to help them build a vocabulary of feeling
words so they can recognize, name, accept, and express their emotions. While grief is a physical phenomenon, children still need
words in order to communicate what they are feeling to other

people. Say what you see a child doing and leave it to him or her to tell you what he or she is feeling. For example, "I see a boy [girl] stomping his feet. You're so full of feelings right now. I'm wondering if you're feeling frustrated or disappointed? Or maybe confused?" Such conversation serves several purposes:

- You are acknowledging that you see the child and what he or she is doing. He or she still exists.
- You are making no mistakes by mislabeling and assuming what the child's feeling is.
- You are providing the child with feelings words, and he or she can recognize and name one that fits or use another one. You are expanding vocabulary by teaching new words.
- You are showing that you accept his or her emotions and are willing to talk about them. You model that it is all right to talk about feelings and death.
- You are affirming and accepting your child's need to express feelings.

Conversation Tips

Communicate honestly and often.	"Would you like to talk about . . . ?" "Is now a good time to talk?"
Share your own memories.	"I remember when my grandma died. . . ."
Show that you are listening.	"Uh-huh," "Hmm," "I see," "Okay"
Affirm the child's efforts to talk.	"I'm so glad you told me about that." "Tell me more."
Clear up confusion.	"I'm not sure I understand . . . is this what you mean?"
Echo feeling statements.	Child: "I was really mad when Daddy drove away."
	Adult: "You felt very mad when your dad left."
Identify feelings and increase vocabulary.	"I'm wondering if you're feeling . . . ?"
Share your own feelings.	"This is what happened for me. I felt really abandoned when my mother died and she couldn't be at my birthday parties anymore."

23

Social Rituals

Funerals, memorial services, wakes, visitations, and other rituals model for children how their family and their culture mourns. Different cultures follow different traditions. If the child's family follows a particular religious tradition, that too will have its own rituals. These rituals provide a time and place for mourning and can be comforting to those who attend. They also show children that mourning is not only an individual experience, but also a family or group experience that can be shared.

Give children a choice about attending

Children need to be offered choices about attending social rituals. Attending such a ritual can help them say good-bye and will help them accept the reality of death. However, do not force them to go if they don't want to.

Explain what takes place at any ritual and what kind of behavior is expected or exhibited. Does the child have to sit quietly, will there be singing or story telling, will people cry, will there be a body, and so on. Tell who will be at the service and when and where it will be.

The child's age is not the most important factor in whether or not to attend. Ask more than once about going to the service as a child may change his or her mind, even at the last minute. Respect the child's decision and make sure someone is available to stay with the child if he or she decides to remain at home.

Many people who have suffered the loss of someone ask another caring adult to be in charge of young children who are going to attend a funeral because it can be hard to concentrate on the service and control fidgety children at the same time.

Invite children to help plan a service

Most children appreciate being included in planning a service. Ask their opinions and ideas about how to honor the person who has died. Tell them what sort of decisions have to be made: music, flowers, prayers, readings, photographs from the person's life, refreshments, and so on.

Let children choose keepsakes

Offer your children the chance to choose a keepsake from the possessions of their loved one who has died or moved away. Such keepsakes represent the emotional relationship the child had with the person. Any object that is significant to the child can become a treasured memento. Possibilities are jewelry, clothing, lock of hair, tools or recreational equipment, books, plants, photos.

As Time Passes

Anniversaries

The anniversary of a death or divorce can be a significant marker. Do not expect that you or your children will be feeling better or farther along in reconciling and accepting the loss.

Take time to honor the anniversary. Many families plan an anniversary ceremony of remembrance by visiting the cemetery, lighting a candle, planting a tree, or going on a walk of remembrance. Tears are to be expected, and children can continue to experience random physical and emotional grief impulses. Ceremonies of remembrance acknowledge that the relationship between the child and the person has changed, not ended.

When to Get More Help

Grieving can take years. Regardless of how long ago the loss happened in your child's life, you cannot ignore the effect it has on your child's overall development. Sometimes the effects are extreme and your concerns are serious.

Most children display grief in behavior. While some behavior can be unsettling to adults, most of the behavior is normal. However, if your child's behavior impacts day-to-day life in a negative way or is harmful to the child or others, you need to act immediately.

Help from a professional

Most grieving children will benefit from the attention of a professional counselor. Get names of people who have worked successfully with children from your pediatrician, clergy, and other knowledgeable people. At your initial meeting, ask for documentation that describes the counselor's training and experience, what the fees are, and how the counseling process works. This is your opportunity to decide if you feel comfortable and confident that

27

this person can help you and your child. Also, check with your child's pediatrician to be sure that there are no physical problems that might be causing worrisome behavior.

A children's grief support group also helps. Being among other children who are grieving is very supportive.

Severe circumstances

Children who have had lives in which they experienced many and frequent losses can develop serious problems. For any child, a loss that is sudden and unexpected will make grieving more difficult. Also, a child who *witnesses* a death—car accident, suicide, natural disaster, heart attack, drowning—can have a more traumatic response. And any child whose emotional or mental health was unstable before a major loss of any kind can react in a more profound and complicated way. Knowing your child's grief and loss history can alert you to the possible need for professional help.

Loss of skill or competence

As children grow they naturally gain skills. Once in a while, when they are concentrating on developing a new skill, other established skills will fade briefly. A grieving child, however, can suffer drastic, sudden loss of skills. This is grief. If the situation doesn't improve and you become more concerned, seek professional help.

Extreme responses

Following are four areas where a child's extreme reaction to grief and loss can show up. Any of these signs, or any combination of them *over a period of weeks or months*, may indicate a need for professional help.

Physical signs

Increase or decrease in appetite

Disturbances or changes in sleep

Increase or decrease in weight

Stomach or headaches, nausea

More frequent illness or injury

Carelessness or disregard for personal safety

Changes in toileting habits

Extreme activity or no activity at all

Dirty or sloppy appearance, or disregard for appearance

Social signs

New fears of strangers

Aggression, hurting self or others or injuring animals

Setting fires

Insisting on taking care of others

Overly passive, withdrawn, quiet

Very defiant, uncooperative

Destruction of property

Increased need for control

Self-blame or blame of others

Not getting along with others

Avoiding talk about grief

Alcohol or drug abuse

Belief that he or she won't live long

Extra watchful and wary

Emotional response

Showing feelings in unusual ways, or showing no feelings at all

New fears

Seeing, hearing, feeling, smelling things that do not exist

Thinking and talking about suicide

Feeling very guilty

Angry or hostile all the time

Fearful, panicky, anxious all the time

Easily surprised

Trying to relieve stress by picking at himself, twiddling or pulling hair, sucking or biting lips, masturbating

Wide mood swings that do not match the situation, joyful one minute and angry the next

Intellectual or skill-based response

Lack of interest in hobbies or general activities

Reduced self-esteem and self-confidence

Confused thinking

Forgetfulness

Loss of skills already mastered

Concerns about or trouble in school

Shorter attention span

Overly competent or self-reliant

Taking on adult care roles

Increased incompetence or helplessness

Tips for Using the Activities

What to expect

All the activities in this book have value for a grieving child.
(Adults may benefit also.) Plan to do whichever activity you choose
with your child; invite other children to do the activity as well.
Mourning is a community event: grieving people draw comfort from
being together.

Expect to try several activities before you find the one that is
just right at the moment. Some of the activities are messy, so pick
a location in your home where you can leave the activity out or can
clean up easily.

Once your child seems drawn to a particular activity and is benefitting from it, allow him or her to repeat it as often or as long as
desired. Some activities can even be broken into smaller pieces
and used over a long time, such as making the Memory Book. Let
the child direct how the activity goes, and stop when the child
wishes to.

Timing and communication

Give your child plenty of time to explore the activity and try not to
direct or interrupt him or her.

Be flexible and monitor your child's pace. Be aware of the feeling tone and energy level of your child. When he or she wants to
stop, stop.

Say what you see your child doing with his or her body, face, and eyes. Use position words, such as, "I see a girl [boy] putting a rock on top of the pile."

Offer feeling words, and avoid labeling the child's feeling yourself. Increase the number of different feeling words you use in conversation so that your child hears new words. Look at page 23, "Conversation Tips," for supportive ways to talk with grieving children.

Getting ready

Reduce as much as possible the number of distractions by turning off television, radio, and telephone, and by arranging for as much peace as possible wherever you are doing an activity.

Read over the activity directions before you begin and make any adjustments your particular circumstance calls for. Gather recommended supplies before beginning an activity.

Have confidence that as you become familiar with these simple activities, they will be a regular, natural part of your care for your grieving child.

Keeping Children Safe

All children need to feel safe, and this is particularly true for grieving children. Due to the powerful emotional and physical tone of childhood grief, adults need to pay special attention to promote emotional security and physical safety. One of the most effective ways to do this is to be present while your child does activities. You will then be aware of your child's behavior and emotional expressions.

Insuring emotional security

The activities in this book are aimed at helping children express themselves and release grief energy. Occasionally, you may notice that your child needs to take a break or rest for a short time in order to pace his or her emotional reactions during an activity. Sometimes, a child may need to stop an activity altogether, possibly returning to it at a later time.

It is important to your child's emotional security for you to respect and honor your child's unique pace and desires during a time of grief. You can be extremely reassuring when you encourage your child to rest or stop as he or she feels the need.

Tell your child that it is all right to:
- Slow down
- Watch for a bit
- Rest for a minute
- Stop for a time

In some cases, a child may benefit from watching as other children take part in an activity. Even though the child is on the sidelines watching, he or she is still involved and benefitting from the activity.

33

Insuring physical safety

Many of the activities in this book use the large muscles of the body to release physical grief energy. These activities provide a deliberate way to release explosive, pent-up grief energy in a healthy manner.

As with any activity involving use of large muscles, unintended mishaps can occur. To assure to the best of your ability that no one gets hurt, monitor the activities carefully by being present yourself. Remind your child to be gentle physically—no hitting, striking, kicking of self or others. State clearly that you will stop the activity if anyone feels or looks unsafe.

If someone gets hurt

If at any time someone's feelings or body gets hurt, stop the activity and attend to the child. You may not always be able to see the hurt, but it can nevertheless be real to the child. Bandage what is visible and cuddle your child with blanket or teddy bear in a rocking chair. Take the time to look for other wounds using a cotton ball and calm your child with understanding hugs and kisses.

If one child accidently hurts another, facilitate an apology. Accidents can be powerful learning experiences for grieving children who have suffered loss due to accidental causes. Your child has a chance to accept that accidents sometimes cause small injury to someone, and sometimes great injury.

Activity Symbols

Each activity has a symbol that tells you at a glance what the activity is useful for. To decide what activity to choose, gather clues from your child's behavior. For example, if she bites her nails constantly, maybe choose a small muscle activity; if she stomps her feet, possibly a large muscle activity. Be careful not to jump to conclusions about some "psychological" meaning to a child's behavior. Instead, see it as grief energy moving naturally through a child's body.

Each of the five groups of activities starts with a short introduction, "Before You Begin." The information in these introductions is important to ensure the success and safety of each activity.

Person to person connections address the urgent need to form close associations with other people and to build trust. A child needs times to be with people who remain after a death or divorce and to construct a new "picture" of his or her changed life, just as adults do. Try one of these nurturing activities.

Soothing repetitive activities include motions repeated over and over. These activities help children create a rhythm to cope with the flood of grief energy. If you see your child rocking, curled up in ball, staring off into space, or going off alone, try one of these activities.

Ceremonies, keepsakes, and memorials address the need to create something to represent or symbolize the loss of a person or pet. These activities may help a child talk about his or her feelings and what the chosen symbol means. Often these activities are a craft and the child must use small muscles to create the symbol, by using markers, scissors, clay, etc.

Large muscle activities address the need to release grief energy through the large muscles of arms, legs, and back. If you see what looks like aggressive, angry behavior, try one of these activities.

Small muscle activities address the need to release grief energy through the small muscles of the hands, fingers, and face. If you see a child ringing hands, biting fingernails, pulling or twiddling hair, picking at clothes or things, making grimaces or looking anxious, try one of these activities.

Part Two

Five Essential Ways to Help Grieving Children

Person to Person Connections

Before You Begin

Children develop a mental picture of their world based on interactions with other people. And they see *themselves* through the eyes of other people. When a loved one dies or moves due to divorce, the child's picture changes. Life no longer exists as it used to; the child may even feel *he* or *she* ceases to exist. This is because their mental picture of reality is shattered.

Grief is the process of accepting and resolving the changes

in the mental picture. Eventually, through interactions with those who remain, a child begins to form a new picture. For this to occur, children need people who are present and available to them. Those who care for grieving children help children make new pictures that reflect the change in their circumstances.

There are many ways to be present and available to children. A nurturing hug, a hand massage, combing hair, a quiet conversation all help children accept change. Make-believe play is especially helpful because through it a child can reenact the event that changed his or her life and explore how the new life is.

1

Hand Massage

Touch has a powerful effect on people, especially those who have suffered a loss. One of the most helpful forms of touch is massage. One of the easiest massages to do is on the hands. Many nerves are located in the hands and are affected by the flow of grief energy. When you rub a child's hand rhythmically, grief energy flows away and your child may be more comfortable. Even simply holding hands can be comforting.

Always ask your child's permission to touch his or her hand before you begin this activity. If your child says no, then try a different activity.

Supplies

Hand lotion, massage oil, or vegetable oil

Directions

1. Before you begin, read the instructions that follow and then explain to your child what you're going to do.

40

2. Find out how the child likes to be touched: stroke the hand lightly first, then more firmly. Ask the child which touch he or she likes better.
3. Put lotion or oil on the child's palm.
4. Grasp the child's hand, palm up, placing your thumb on the palm and your fingers underneath.
5. Starting at the wrist, move your thumb in a circular motion across the palm to the base of the fingers. Do this over and over, covering the whole palm, until the child tires of it.
6. Turn the child's hand over and apply more oil or lotion.
7. Next, massage each finger, beginning with the child's thumb. Support the child's hand with your fingers on the palm and your thumb free to move on top of the child's hand.
8. Start massaging the child's thumb first, beginning at the wrist again. Follow the bone line, moving your thumb in a circular motion and holding the thumb between your thumb and fingers, downward to the end of the thumb. Concentrate on the joints where grief energy can build up.
9. Repeat with each finger.
10. Complete your massage by going over the whole hand, from wrist to finger tips, with both of your hands. Put your

thumbs on the top of the child's hand and your fingers on the palm. Slide your hands very gently (so as not to dislocate weak shoulder and elbow joints in children) down the child's palm and then make a fist around each finger and thumb in turn and gently pull your fist down to the tip and off. You and your child can imagine that you are pulling unwanted feelings out of the fingers and letting them go.

11. Repeat the process with the child's other hand.

Variation

- Massage your child's feet in the same manner.

2

Playing Beauty Shop or Barber Shop

Many of the care-taking tasks parents do with their children, such as washing and combing hair, are beneficial during times of loss. Playing "Beauty Shop" or "Barber Shop" offers a child an opportunity to be physically close to an adult. The rhythmic, soothing motion of brushing hair or "shaving" skin and the chance to gaze at oneself in the mirror help a child feel more emotionally anchored.

Supplies

Comb and brush
Shampoo
Towels
Hair rollers
Mirror
Hair dryer
Whipped cream
Popsicle sticks (pretend razor)

Directions

Option #1: Beauty Shop

1. Decide who will be the stylist and who will be the client. Adult and child can take turns being both.
2. Wash the client's hair, taking time to massage the scalp gently. Dry off with the towel.
3. Have the client sit in a low chair or on the floor in front of the couch with the hairstylist/barber standing or sitting behind.
4. Give client the mirror. Comb or brush the client's hair slowly and gently.
5. Blow dry the hair, running hands through the hair at the same time.
6. Talk to each other about anything you feel like, if you want to. Sometimes this is an opportunity to share reflections about the person who died or moved away, or about the pet that died.

44

7. Put the client's hair in rollers. Blow dry and then comb out the curls.
8. Repeat the activity often, daily if needed.

Option #2: Barber Shop

1. Use all the steps above and add the following.
2. Put whipping cream or vanilla pudding on the client's chin (male or female) and have the barber pretend to shave off the cream with a popsicle stick.
3. Put whipping cream or vanilla pudding on the client's legs (male or female) below the knees and have the barber pretend to shave it off.

Variation

- You can do a similar nurturing activity using children's washable make-up or face paint. Boys will enjoy the activity if you explain that both male and female actors in movies and on stage use make-up and many actors have their faces painted to resemble animals or make-believe characters.

3

Breathing and Visualization

Sometimes, seemingly out of nowhere, a waterfall of grief energy wells up. Children need skills to manage this energy, which may include a powerful impulse to cry. One of the most helpful of these is to learn how to breathe rhythmically in response to a surge of emotion. Being able to create a calming visual image to focus on is another skill. These skills can be used together or separately to help the child cope.

Supplies

None

Directions

1. As soon after a loss as you can, explain to your child that he or she may have feelings that seem overwhelming. He or she may feel like crying. Tell your child that there are two things to do when such overwhelming feelings come: deep breathing and visualization.

2. Teach your child how to do deep breathing:
    Put both hands over the belly button.
    Breathe in through the nose to fill the lungs. The child
      should be able to see his or her hands move.
    Exhale through the mouth. The child's abdomen should
      visibly sink inward.
3. Spend as much time as necessary to help your child learn
    how to do this kind of rhythmical breathing.
4. Once your child can do deep breathing then teach him or
    her how to do visualization. Talk about something wonder-
    ful the child could see in his or her imagination and how
    this image can help to calm him or her. Or follow the steps
    below.
5. Encourage your child to combine deep breathing with
    visualization.

Suggested visualization

1. Ask your child to close his or her eyes and pretend to be
    in a small boat on a calm river.
2. Suggest that he or she picture him- or herself drifting down
    the quiet river in the boat. (Other people can come along,
    if the child desires.)
3. Encourage your child to breathe deeply and relax as he or

she drifts slowly down the peaceful river.

4. After drifting quietly for a while, suggest that your child imagine him- or herself moving to shore and getting out of the boat, walking slowly to a comfortable spot to rest.

Note: If the child's loss happened because someone drowned, do not use this visualization. Substitute a walk through a sunny meadow instead.

4

Play Acting

Through play acting (make believe) children symbolically develop an understanding of their world and how it works. Since grieving is a physical process, it is helped along when children physically play out their grief.

During play acting your child is in charge of what happens. Anything he or she wishes to act out is all right as long as no one is being hurt. Your role is to be present and join in if possible. Let your child direct your role. By *repeating* the play the child begins to fold the loss into a new mental picture of him- or herself and the changed situation.

Supplies

Stuffed toys, action figures, dolls
Puppets
Clothing for costumes
Any kind of prop that might enhance the play acting

Directions

Option #1: When the child has begun to play act

1. Watch to see what the play is that your child has begun. Look for a role you might play.
2. Ask, "May I play with you?" If the answer is yes, ask, "What can I be?" Slowly begin to speak a few words and add actions that fit what your child tells you. If you are not given a role, then try one you think might work.
3. Follow your child's directions as to how to play. Ask the child to show you what to do if you're not sure what he or she wants. Make believe in which the child is in charge may give him or her a beneficial feeling of control.
4. If your child says no to your joining the play, then just be present and be still. It helps grieving children to have people "see" them, to confirm their continued existence. You can also watch for safety issues.
5. If you see a role is missing in the child's play—for

example, a hospital scene in which the child is a doctor but there is no patient—play the part of the patient or offer a toy that can fill that role (or any other).

6. Continue play acting as long as possible.

Option #2: When the child is not play acting but you sense it would be helpful

1. Ask your child if he or she would like to play.
2. Ask if he or she has ideas of what to play and what you can each be.
3. Suggest some low-key ideas, such as: teacher and student; kitten and mother cat or puppy and mother dog; people in a grocery store; veterinarian caring for animals; race car driver; firefighter getting a kitten out of a tree; chef cooking a feast for family and friends.
4. Your goal is to get play acting started and then to follow your child's lead as above in choice #1.

Option #3: When child is play acting, but play appears repetitive with no obvious acting, no development of story or situation. For example, a child might be looking in a mirror and combing her hair over and over.

1. Be present, be still. Watch your child.

2. Say what you see happening: "I see a girl combing her hair. Her hair is black. She is using a blue comb." In this way, you are helping your child begin to see herself as alive even if she doesn't feel so because she is numb with grief.
3. When the child's actions change, say what you see, as in step 2.

Option #4: For any of the above situations, use a puppet and let the child talk for it.

5

Building Trust in the Future

Children thrive when life is predictable. When they suffer loss, their sense of security and ability to trust are shaken. Sometimes they may be worried about who will take care of them and do all the other things they need. You can reassure your child by talking about changes openly. Try to maintain your child's routine as much as possible. Avoid moving to a new house or school if you can. If big changes are unavoidable, talking about them is a must. Explain what will change and what will remain the same.

Supplies

Paper, pens, markers

Directions

1. Observe your child and decide what time of day he or she would be most able to cope with a discussion about routines and schedules.

2. Give your child advance notice that you want to talk about his or her daily schedule.
3. At the time you decide, take the phone off the hook and turn off other distractions. Gather the supplies listed above.
4. Sit down with your child and say, for example, "Since Grandpa died, we have had several changes around here. Do you remember that last Saturday you could not go to the zoo with him and last Wednesday Aunt Sophie took you to soccer practice instead of Grandpa?" Choose simple terms to describe whatever changes your child is dealing with. Ask your child what changes he or she has noticed. It's all right if the child gives no answer.
5. Tell your child that you are going to write out his or her daily schedule so that you can both remember what is going to happen and who is going to do it. Make a list like the following, tailored to your child's particular routine.

My Schedule

_____ *wakes me up and helps me get dressed in the morning.*

_____ *makes my breakfast and packs my lunch.*

_____ *takes me to school.*

_____ *picks me up from school.*

After school I go _____.

_____ *fixes my dinner.*

_____ *helps me with my homework and reminds me about my chores.*

_____ *helps me with my bath.*

_____ *tucks me into bed, reads me a story, and turns on the night-light.*

I see my counselor at _____ *on* _____.

6. Put this list on your refrigerator and inside your child's school notebook. Any time the routine changes, tell your child immediately and revise both lists.

7. Hold family meetings on the weekend to talk about the upcoming week and make a new list as needed.

Variations

- Make a list of first and last names and phone numbers with area codes of people in your child's life, such as relatives, neighbors, teachers, and professionals, who are willing and available to offer reassurance or other help as needed.

- Write out a safety plan for various types of emergencies: what to do if lost, hurt, or feeling ill; what to do in case of lost house key or pet; etc.

Soothing Repetitive Activities

Before You Begin

Grief often has an intense physical affect on the body. Brain, muscles, and internal organs work together to understand the loss. These physical sensations of grief come and go in random, unpredictable impulses. Any repetitive motion can help regulate the flow of random energy.

Repetitive motion replicates the natural heartbeat and the regular rhythm of breathing. The goal of repetitive motion is to move grief energy through the body at a regular pace, in the same manner as the heart and lungs function. A child will feel more comfortable and less tense, and in some cases may be more likely to talk about his or her grief. Any activity repeated over and over counts as repetitive motion—bouncing or tossing a ball, filling and pouring water in the sink or bathtub, rocking, jumping rope, tracing a pattern in the sand. Children who have skill playing an instrument may play the same song over and over.

Rocking Chair Connection

Rocking in a rocking chair provides a comforting rhythm for a grieving child. If the child is agitated or upset or angry, rocking can calm and soothe.

Supplies

One or more rocking chairs
Quiet environment without distractions
Comforting "lovey" or stuffed animal, blanket, or other object for child to hold

Directions

1. Pick a time to rock as part of each day's routine.
2. Hold the child in your lap and rock or each sit in your own rocking chair and rock companionably.
3. Be quiet if the child doesn't want to talk, or talk quietly as long as that is comforting to your child.
4. Decide how long to rock; be consistent each day.

7

Sand and Water Play

The textures, sensations, and sounds of playing in sand and water are infinitely soothing to grieving children. The repetitive motions of scooping and pouring sand and water create a pace to regulate the random impulses of grief energy. As children build structures with sand and water they see change. That change mirrors what may be happening in their lives. Sand-and-water play encourages play acting (page 49) in which children may begin to talk about their loss.

Supplies

Sand play
Sand box outdoors or a large plastic dish tub inside
Fine sand, available at building supply stores
Glitter and sequins (optional)
Plastic toys, including people and animals
Plastic cups and utensils
Toy hand tools

Broom and dustpan for indoor clean-up

Water play
Large plastic dish tub or bathtub
Bubble bath (optional)
Plastic containers and strainer
Plastic toys, including people and animals
Large paintbrush
Mop for indoor clean-up

Directions

1. Prepare the play area for your child's choice of activity.
2. Let your child play as long as he or she wishes. Supervise for safety, especially around water!
3. Join in play acting if your child wishes you to (page 49).
4. Make a game of clean-up when play time is over.

Variation

- Mix sand and water in the dish tub for making sand structures.

8

Round and Round with Marbles

As a child stirs marbles around in a bowl, grief energy is released. Handling different and interesting textures also helps as it stimulates the nerve endings in the fingers. Listening to calming familiar music may be beneficial, too.

Supplies

Marbles of all sizes, colors, and patterns
Wooden or plastic bowl to fit in child's lap
Quiet location and rocking chair or other comfortable place to sit
Pillow and blanket
Teddy bear or other treasured toy
Soothing music in background

Directions

1. Seat your child comfortably. Offer to wrap him or her up in the blanket; place the pillow and toy close by, as your

child wishes. Turn on the music.

2. Put the bowl of marbles in your child's lap.

3. Tell your child to roll the marbles around in the bowl (or stir with a wooden spoon) and at the same time to imagine a wonderful place where he or she could feel peaceful. Maybe this is a beach, or forest, or the grass in the backyard. Maybe it is rocking in a boat on calm water or riding a bike in the sunshine.

4. As your child rolls marbles and visualizes a calm place, tell him or her to breathe in deeply through the nose and exhale slowly through the mouth.

5. Encourage your child to look at all the colors of the marbles and to listen to the noise they make bumping into each other. Let your child continue this activity as long as desired.

Variations

- Use small rocks, beans, rice, macaroni, or buttons instead of marbles. Or place a small treasured keepsake in the bowl for the child to focus on.
- Give a child a "Slinky" to play with or a deck of cards to shuffle over and over.
- Teach your child how to twiddle his or her thumbs. Lace fingers together and lay hands in lap. Roll thumbs around and around each other like the paddle wheel of a steam boat or mill.

Remember to tell your child to do deep breathing and to visualize a wonderful, calm place and to listen to the soft music playing.

9

Ball Play

Many childhood activities that children naturally take part in, like bouncing balls, are not only entertaining but beneficial. As a grieving child's brain and body work together to cope with remarkable transition and change, the repetitive motion of bouncing a ball rhythmically up and down or against a wall helps the child. The bouncing ball provides a meditative focal point that enables a child to relax and reflect on his or her life.

The tempo of a bouncing ball against a wall or on cement establishes a soothing rhythm for the grief energy flowing through the child's body. The goal is to provide an activity that allows for rhythmic motion to deal with grief energy. Competition could be frustrating and is to be avoided.

Supplies

Basketballs or other large balls
(No baseballs or softballs or other balls typically thrown toward other people)

Solid wall without windows, or a cement or paved surface
Basketball court, optional

Directions

1. Gather the balls and head for the play area.
2. Child and adult can bounce balls up and down on the cement or against the wall.
3. Talk as the child feels like it. Answer his or her questions and share memories.
4. Encourage the child to go out and bounce a ball often.

10

Let's Take a Walk

People often take walks when they are coping with strong feelings. They are not escaping from the situation but seem naturally to be drawn to being outdoors. Walking helps them deal with their thoughts and feelings. The repetitive, rhythmic motion of walking helps release grief energy through the large muscles of arms, legs, and back.

Some people find that walking a familiar path, where twists and turns are known, is more relaxing than walking someplace unfamiliar where they must be extra careful. Take your grieving child for a walk along a familiar path often. Even a simple lazy eight pattern in the backyard is beneficial to a grieving child.

Another special kind of place to walk is a *labyrinth*. A labyrinth is a maze-like pathway in the form of a repeating pattern. The drawings show examples. At the center of the labyrinth is often a place to stop and reflect or meditate. Walking a labyrinth provides repetitive motion and a chance to release grief energy. Labyrinths can sometimes be found in parks, churches, and in corn fields in the fall.

Homemade labyrinth

Supplies

Indoor or outdoor space large enough to lay out a
   labyrinthine design
Long rope or flexible garden hose to create the design pattern
Outdoors: pine cones, rocks, branches, rows of raked leaves
   or grass clippings to mark the pathway
Indoors: pillows, stuffed toys, rolled up sheets or blankets,
   masking tape to mark the pathway

Directions

1. Work with your child to design a shape for the labyrinth. (A spiral works well.)
2. Place the rope or hose in the shape you have chosen.

3. To mark the pathway along which to walk, use any of the items gathered. Make two parallel borders on either side of the rope or hose, three feet apart, so that two people can walk side by side or pass one another.
4. Place a large stone at the center to mark a place to stop and reflect.
5. Encourage your child to walk the labyrinth over and over, stopping at the center for as long as he or she wishes to remember their loss.

Variation

- Mow a labyrinthine shape in your lawn or field.

Ceremonies, Keepsakes, and Memorials

Before You Begin

Grief is the process of accepting the finality of death or divorce. It takes time to absorb the fact that the person or pet will never come back again or that the parent who has moved will not return home. Grief also is the process of forming memories about the person or pet and the relationship as it was.

By honoring the relationship that existed before death or divorce in a formal way, through choosing a keepsake, holding a ceremony, funeral, or memorial service, or creating a memorial, children have a visual way to remember that the relationship they had was *real*. It also helps them see and accept the reality that life is different now.

There is a saying that "what the eye can see, the heart can remember." When a death or divorce occurs, a child suffers a visual loss because he or she can no longer see the person or pet. Creating something visual or choosing a keepsake expands the child's capacity to think about and remember a loved one.

11

Ceremonies

Ceremonies, funerals, memorial services, or other rituals are often public expressions of love, remembrance, and intimacy among people. They help people reflect on the times and the loss and provide opportunities for people to gather together in community to mourn.

Whenever there is a death, people who knew that person have a need to get together to honor and remember him or her. Elements of a ritual engage all five senses: sight, sound, smell, taste, and touch. These elements create powerful memories that children and adults can recall all their lives. Involving children in the planning of a ceremony offers them choices at a time when they have very little control over what is happening in their lives.

As time goes by, holding ceremonies honoring the person's birthday and remembering him or her on holidays and on the anniversary of his or her death will help children structure their feelings. Children will need adult help in the future on these dates to reflect, recall, and remember. People need these repeated opportunities to recall and remember the person who has died.

There are three kinds of ceremonies or rituals that help grieving children:

- *Formal community service* that occurs shortly after the person's death. Usually anyone who knew the person may attend to reflect and remember.

- *Intimate repeated ceremonies* that families hold as time passes, to honor the special days, such as birthday, anniversary of death, holidays, and any other special days.
- *Play-acting ceremonies* (make believe) children may be naturally drawn to conduct on their own in which they may reenact ceremonies they have attended soon after the death. (See page 49.)

There is as much value in the gathering of ideas and the planning of ceremonies as there is in conducting and taking part in them. Both provide children with choices that help them feel more secure during a time of loss. Include them as much as their age and stage of development will allow.

If a child's loss is through divorce or death of a pet, consider having a ceremony of remembrance or funeral at home. Use the suggestions that follow to structure the ceremony you can hold together to remember and honor the loss.

Elements

Place to gather
Invited family and/or friends
Decorations (flowers, balloons, etc.)
Music, sung, played, or recorded
Photographs of the person or pet

Tokens of remembrance, such as a program or drawing
Candles
Words to say, such as a poem, story, letter, or memories
Prayer or blessing
Burial place for the pet

Directions

1. Decide on and prepare the burial place if the child is honoring a pet that has died.
2. Plan the ceremony of loss or death using the elements suggested above and any others of importance to your child. Based on your experience as an adult with ceremonies of remembrance, you can help your child structure the beginning, middle, and end of the ceremony.
3. After the ceremony is finished, offer all participants some refreshments suited to their tastes. Children may prefer something different from what adults would expect.
4. Thank everyone who gathered for the ceremony for attending and helping to remember and recall the person who is gone or the pet that has died.

12

Balloons Afloat

The act of releasing a helium balloon can be a powerful symbolic ceremony for a grieving child. The child decides when to let the balloon go—until that moment he or she is in control of the event. As the child watches the released balloon float into the air, eventually to disappear, it can represent visually the person who was in the child's life and now is gone. In a sense, the child relives the experience of the loved one's departure or death, but in an expected or planned way.

Supplies

Several helium-filled balloons or balloons to blow up
Markers, paper, tape, string

Directions
Planning

1. Explain to your child that you are planning a ceremony to help him or her with feelings of grief.

2. Together choose a special place (park, beach, field, or the burial site) and a date and time to release the balloons.
3. Prepare for the ceremony by selecting music or words to read at that time. Sometimes, the releasing of balloons is part of a funeral or memorial service; it can also be done at other times and as many times as desired.
4. Consider inviting other people to share the ceremony.
5. On the day of the ceremony, gather everyone at the special place, with a quantity of helium-filled balloons. Be prepared for a variety of emotions and behavior, from running and stomping to clinging and crying. If any balloons break before release, pause to deal with any feelings the child has (he or she may be very upset).

Ceremony

6. Let everyone present compose notes or think of words they would like to write on or attach to the balloons before they are released if they wish. Help the children do this task so they are easily successful.
7. While everyone is still holding their balloon(s), talk about how loss and change are natural in life, and can be painful. Talk about the balloon representing the child's loved one or pet. Say that you are all going to let your balloons float

away into the sky where they will disappear from view, just as the child's loved one disappeared. Remind the child that he or she can remember what the balloon looks like as it floats away, perhaps carrying a message for a loved one, and he or she can remember the loved person too.

8. Release the balloons into the air and watch them float away.
9. Play music, read verses, or do other planned quiet activities as the balloons disappear.
10. When the balloons are gone, offer comfort by hugging or holding hands.

13

Keepsakes

Keepsakes, or mementos, represent a child's emotional relationship to the person or pet who has died or to the person who has moved out. Such a keepsake can bring to mind powerful memories and feelings. Children may treasure owning something that belonged to the person they miss. When they hold the keepsake or look at it, they are better able to accept the loss and look toward the future. They may also feel that some part of that person or pet is still with them and be comforted.

Setting

Adult and child in the presence of the loved one's possessions: the person's home or a box of items from which the child may choose

Directions

1. Set aside a quiet, uninterrupted time to talk with your

child about choosing a keepsake. Explain that having a keepsake to look at or hold is often comforting. It helps a child remember the loved one and helps the child with his or her feelings of grief.

2. Choose a day that will be calm and not too full of other stressful activities (such as tests at school or a doctor's appointment). Decide whether the people choosing keepsakes should do so individually or in a group.

3. If the person who died left certain things to other people, be sure those things are not in sight when your child chooses a keepsake. Also, do not assume that the child will be satisfied by what the dead person left him or her— your child may treasure something quite different.

4. If your child doesn't want to choose a keepsake, you may choose several items you think might be treasured and put them away for the child to consider at another time.

5. Prepare yourself for the fact that what your child chooses may seem an odd choice to you and may be different from what another child might choose. Respect your child's choice. If allowed, help your child choose more than one item and think what your child might like at different stages in the future as he or she remembers. A fishing pole might suit the ten-year-old, but at 25 he or she may enjoy

Grandma's favorite cookbook or Uncle John's favorite volume of poetry.

6. The size of a keepsake can be important. Something small can be carried around or worn; something large, like a blanket or favorite chair, can cuddle the child.

7. Plan how the child is going to look after the keepsake. Be aware that he or she may be greatly distressed if it is lost. Decide together how, when, and where the keepsake can be used. Let other grown-ups know about the keepsake so they understand the emotional value of it.

Variations

- Give the child one of the keepsakes chosen for him or her on special occasions or anniversaries on which you remember the person who died.

- If the person who died lived far away, call and ask the executor if the things your child asked about could be set aside for him or her and shipped.

- Choose keepsakes for your child even if he or she did not know the person who died well. As children grow they are naturally curious about relatives, especially, and a keep-sake can be meaningful as family connection.

- Remember to think about choosing items of religious or

cultural significance. Such items contribute to a child's sense of identity as he or she grows.

Note: Your child may not desire a keepsake from the possessions of the person who died or moved. He or she may respond more to a furry friend of some sort (nonliving). Teddy bears, for example, are a universal symbol of hope and love. All over the world teddy bears are given to children when they are hurt, ill, or grieving.

Whether your child likes a bear or some other stuffed toy, the benefits for comfort are:

- Its face looks understanding, as if it knew what the child feels.
- It is soft. By holding it tenderly, a child can imagine being held tenderly.
- Whatever the child says to the toy is accepted without comment or criticism.

- The toy will stay with the child as long as it is needed.
- It can be a symbolic representation that the child is grieving.

Some children may feel they are too old to need a stuffed toy, but when a child or teenager is grieving, the warmth and understanding of a quiet teddy bear may help. Consider pulling out favorite toys from childhood, too.

14

Painted Rock Memorial

Ancient peoples painted rocks or cave walls to record their histories. Their sorrows and pleasures were represented by the symbols they chose. In Japan there is a tradition of painting rocks and wrapping them with string for good luck. There, they place the tied-up rocks inside and outside the doors to their homes. Your child can paint rocks as a memorial to the person or pet, to express grief and hope of a new beginning, and as a means of managing grief energy.

Supplies

Paint that dries permanently, in as many colors as possible (acrylics are a good choice)

Paintbrushes

Rocks of all shapes and sizes

Paper towel or newspaper
Empty can for water
Paper plate on which to mix paint
Twine or string

Directions

1. Wash and dry the rocks.
2. Spread newspaper or paper towel out where the mess won't be a problem.
3. Place the rocks to be painted on the paper.
4. Invite your child to paint the rocks in solid colors or designs of his or her choice. Let your child take as much time as he or she wishes.
5. When the rocks are dry, wrap string around each one.

Variation

• Paint the rocks with water instead of paint. Let them dry and do it again.

15

Memory Book

Making a memory book helps children connect with the memory of a pet or a loved who died or moved away. Such a book provides a way for the child's eyes to anchor the lost one in heart and mind. A memory book may contain any items that are important to the child, like letters, pictures, cards, drawings, pet collar and tags, lock of hair, and so on. You can help a child who is too young to write (or who can't write easily) to add memory pages of text. Your child can dictate to you or you can record memories of your child and the loved one to share with your child.

Making a memory book uses small muscles. Grief energy will be released as a child writes, draws, paints, cuts, and pastes or tapes.

Supplies

Scrapbook containing non-acid paper, available at craft or art supply stores

Special mementos that will fit into a scrapbook
Markers, pens, pencils, watercolor paints
Glue, tape
Stickers, glitter
Decorative paper: foil paper, wallpaper scraps, gift wrapping
Scissors, hole punch
Photographs
Cards received from family and friends

Directions

1. On the first page, put child's name and the date. Put the name, birth date, date of death or departure of the person or pet being honored.
2. On pages of non-acid paper, draw, paint, glue mementos and photos, and decorate generally as the child's creativity and feelings desire.
3. Write memories and stories about the person or pet on some pages.
4. Save some blank pages for adding to the memory book later, as long as the child is interested.

Suggestions for story memories (can be written or drawn)

Favorite memory

Most upsetting memory

How the person or pet died

About the funeral or memorial service

Things you wonder about

Questions you would like to have asked the person

What you honor most about the person

A letter telling the person or pet what you are doing now

A poem about how you feel

Something the person taught you (a skill or an outlook)

A list of all the feeling words that describe how you feel in your mind and in your body

What you do when feelings are very strong or overwhelming

Description of how your life has changed

What makes you feel powerful and in charge of your life

Variation

- A child can make a Memory Box too, which can contain things that relate to the person or pet that is gone. It can hold small treasures and can be decorated as the child wishes. Unfinished wooden boxes are sold at craft stores, but any kind of sturdy box will work. Provide pretty paper, fabric, and stickers, plus markers and paints, for decorating the box. Make as many boxes as needed.

Large Muscle Activities

Before You Begin

Angry, aggressive-seeming body motions are one of the most common behaviors in grieving children. Grief energy moves through the body flooding large muscles with impulses and memories. Children need to use the large muscles in their backs, arms, and legs to cope with this kind of energy.

Any feeling that is intense and unfamiliar can frighten a child. Some children have little experience that would result in such intense feelings. They need adults around who understand what is happening and who can help them to recognize, name, accept, and express their feelings.

Children often feel angry at the person who died or who moved out. They often feel angry at themselves, too, thinking they are somehow responsible. And they can feel angry with some of the adults around them for the same reason.

Some behavior, such as hitting others or throwing toys, looks like the child is expressing anger when she or he may not be. Remember that your child may not have the words to tell you precisely what is going on. All you need to observe is that the child is using big muscles. Your job is to step in with a big-muscle activity for the child to do so that the grief energy can be expressed safely.

Instead of interpreting your child's feelings (you may be wrong), just say what you see the child doing. For example, "I see a girl stomping her feet." Be present and available to your child and let him or her know that you are there to keep everyone safe.

When your child has used up all his or her large muscle grief energy and feels "done," be available to reestablish a physical connection with your child with a hug, or an arm around the shoulders, or by holding hands. Your connection to your child helps him or her maintain control.

16

Stomping Feet

The need to stomp, punt, boot, or march can be powerful in grieving children. The large muscles in their legs are saturated with grief energy needing a release. Anytime a grieving child kicks someone else, that is the signal that his or her legs need a safe and effective outlet for grief energy. It is quite possible that the child doesn't have the urge to hurt someone, but just needs to move in a big way. Remember that grieving children may not be able to express themselves in words. Take care of the child or adult who got kicked, require the kicker to apologize (if possible), and then immediately provide an outlet for kicking legs.

Option #1: Stomping

Supplies

None

Directions

1. Choose a safe place indoors or out for a stomping spot.
2. Begin the activity by having the child stand up and move his or her legs in large, exaggerated stomping motions.
3. Tell the child to breathe in deeply through the nose and exhale slowly through the mouth.
4. Say, "I see a boy [girl] stomping his feet." Avoid labeling feelings, just let the child know you are there and available by describing the *actions* you see.
5. Continue as long as the child wishes.
6. When your child is finished, reconnect physically by hugging, placing an arm around his or her shoulders, or holding hands.

Variations

- Provide materials for the child to stomp on: cardboard boxes, paper cups, soda pop cans, bubble wrap, Styrofoam cubes.
- Go on a stomp walk around the neighborhood or yard, or around the house.
- Go to a swimming pool where the child can stomp in the water.

Option #2: Drumming

Supplies

Empty oatmeal boxes
Pots and pans
Wooden spoons
Drums and drumsticks

Directions

All cultures use drums to express feelings on important occasions. Drumming is helpful for grieving children because it uses large muscles, is rhythmic and repetitive, and makes noise. The child can control volume, rhythm, and pace. Give your child something to drum on and let him or her drum as long you can tolerate the sound. Ask your child if you may join in.

17

Gardening

Working the soil can help people who are feeling troubled and sad. Using the large muscles of the body by digging, shoveling, raking, watering, hoisting plants, and toting earth helps to release grief energy through the arms, legs, and back.

Planting a living thing also symbolically represents the renewal of the life cycle. The opportunity to care for a living thing invites a child to build new emotional connections. As the plant grows, it becomes a visual reminder of the child's loss, as well as a marker for the passage of time. Tending a growing plant is a symbol of an on-going relationship and provides many chances for the child to reflect on his or her loss.

Supplies

Small plants or trees
Shovels and rakes
Work gloves
Watering can, bucket, or hose

Wheelbarrow or wagon (for moving plants or dirt)
Or, tarp or old blanket (for dragging plants or dirt around)

Directions

1. Locate the spot where you want to put the plant. Do you want a plant that will grow large or one that will remain small? Will it grow in sunlight or in shade? Water the spot to loosen the soil.

2. Choose a plant at a garden nursery, where you can get advice on plants that are easy to care for, sturdy, long lived, and suited to the spot you have chosen. Consider purchasing a plant that was a favorite of the person who has died or moved away, if it is suited to your spot.
3. Ask the garden nursery staff for written instructions on how to plant and care for the plant you choose.
4. Set the plant by the space where it will be planted and gather the tools needed for the job.
5. Work together with your child to dig the hole. Allow him or her to do as much of the work as possible. Take as much time as you need (hours or days), keeping the plant moist and shaded until it goes into the ground.
6. Encourage your child to use vigorous motions while digging, hauling, and planting in order to release as much grief energy as possible.
7. Follow the instructions for planting, possibly watering the hole before placing the plant in it, loosening the plant's roots, checking the depth of the hole, and holding the plant while your child fills in the dirt around its roots.
8. Stand back and observe your cooperative work, placing an arm around your child's shoulders, holding hands, or

giving her or him a hug to reestablish the physical connection between you.

Variations

- Use this activity as part of a ceremony (see page 69) to honor the child's loss.
- Take a picture of the plant and your child beside it. Repeat on the anniversary, or other special day, as the child and the plant grow.
- Plan repeat ceremonies as the plant grows: when cutting flowers in the spring and summer, harvesting fruit or colorful branches in the fall, applying mulch or bark to protect the plant in the winter, for example.
- Plant in a container if space is limited. Large muscle use is limited, too, in this case, but your child will still have the benefit of planting and caring for a living thing, watching it grow and change and remembering his or her loss.

18

Newspaper Crush and Crumble

Crushing and wadding up newspaper is an activity that uses large, exaggerated arm motions to release grief energy. Like raking piles of leaves, this activity allows the same vigorous arm motions. When your child tires of the activity, have him or her collect the wadded-up newspaper in a large, heavy plastic garbage bag. You can save it for other activities, like stomping (page 90) or throwing (page 99).

Supplies

A large stack of newspaper
Large plastic garbage bag

Directions

1. Show your child how to pick out one sheet of newspaper and crumble it tightly into a ball using big arm motions. Your child can do this alone or the two of you can do it together, until you have as many balls as possible.

2. Tell your child to breathe in deeply through the nose and exhale slowly through the mouth as he or she makes the newspaper balls.
3. When there is a large quantity of balls, your child can throw them into the plastic garbage bag.
4. Let your child rest when needed and then begin again when he or she wishes.
5. When your child is finished, reconnect physically by hugging, placing an arm around his or her shoulders, or holding hands.

Variation

- A child can tear newspaper or old telephone book pages or magazines.

19

Throwing Balls

Throwing is an action that releases grief energy from the whole body. The goal of throwing balls is to release the grief energy in the arms in a powerful motion. The kind of forceful throwing recommended for grieving children is different from the careful intentional throwing children do when they are trying to develop good aim and control of the ball in team sports. Pick a safe place where your child can throw with all his or her might.

Option #1: Ball Against Wall

Supplies

Balls of all kinds and sizes
Wall without windows to throw against
Safe place where no one and nothing is likely to be hurt

Directions

1. Demonstrate to the child how to throw the ball *hard* against

the wall. This will use most of the child's muscles.

2. Tell the child to breathe in deeply through the nose and exhale slowly through the mouth.

3. Say, "I see a boy [girl] throwing a ball." Avoid labeling feelings, just let the child know you are there and available by describing the *actions* you see.

4. Rotate through all the kinds of balls you have. Your child may settle on a particular ball that feels most satisfying when thrown.

5. When your child is finished, reconnect physically by hugging, placing an arm around his or her shoulders, or holding hands.

Variation

- Use a tennis ball and racquet if the child has the skill.

Option #2: Balloon Volleyball

Supplies

Large number of balloons, blown up
Two people

Directions

1. Pick an open space in which to play safely.

2. Hit a balloon back and forth as vigorously as possible, keeping it in the air. If it breaks, grab another one and keep playing until tired.
3. There are no rules on who "wins." The aim is the release of grief energy.

Option #3: *Balloon Hockey*

Supplies

Large number of balloons, blown up
Two cardboard boxes
Two people

Directions

1. Place a cardboard box at each end of your "playing field" in the house or outdoors.
2. Place a balloon midway between the two boxes.
3. Child and other player get down on hands and knees and hit the balloon toward one of the boxes.
4. Keep playing as long as people are having fun. If a balloon breaks, grab another and keep playing until tired. There are no scores to keep or competition between players. When someone gets the balloon in a box, simply start again.

20

Rock Pile Memorials

Centuries ago nomadic peoples who traveled from place to place without settling down had no cemeteries or graveyards. When one of their group died, they would bury the person and then pile rocks on top of the grave to keep wild animals from digging it up and to mark its location. These rock piles are called cairns (pronounced care-erns, as if it were one syllable).

Building a cairn is an effective way to release grief energy through the large muscles of back, arms, and legs. In addition, when a cairn is finished, the grieving person has a memorial to the loved one who has died or moved or to a favorite pet. Cairns can be built anywhere—at home, in the woods, on the beach, in a park—but you might want to give some thought to a location where the cairn will not be destroyed by other people who don't know of its significance to your child.

Supplies

A large supply of rocks that your child can handle easily

Look for rocks at a plant nursery or gather them from a stream or riverbed.
Gardening or cold weather gloves
Wheelbarrow or wagon

Directions

1. Work with your child to carry the rocks to the place where you have decided to build a cairn.
2. Encourage your child to move his or her body freely and to

breathe in deeply through the nose and exhale slowly through the mouth while stacking the rocks.

3. Rocks can be stacked any which way on top of one another, or your child can place them in a special design. Ask which he or she would like to do, and offer help if the child would like.

4. Let your child toss the rocks into the pile. No one should get hurt, though a falling rock can hurt a finger or toe.

5. Say, "I see a girl [boy] stacking rocks." Avoid labeling feelings, just let the child know you are there and available by describing the *actions* you see.

6. When your child is finished, reconnect physically by hugging, placing an arm around his or her shoulders, or holding hands.

7. After the cairn is finished, visit it as often as the child wishes as a place to remember the person or pet it memorializes. Build it back up again as necessary.

8. As time goes by, return to the cairn to hold repeat ceremonies of remembrance or to release balloons (page 75). Repair the cairn if needed.

Small Muscle Activities

Before You Begin

Creative activities offer children unique ways to express their grief. Art of any description gives children a way to show how they feel without talking. Doing art uses small muscles and releases grief through the hands and fingers. Making something they can see, feel, and touch that represents their memories and feelings gives children a sense of control and power. Doing art or crafts shows a child that he or she does have influence over what's happening, even if only on paper.

You don't need to ask, "What is it?" The process of *doing*

something counts much more than the final product. Your child may or may not tell you. Respect his or her choice.

Always let your child decide what he or she will create and how, with the safe materials you provide. It is more helpful to say, "I see you marking on paper with a yellow marker," than "I see you making a pretty yellow sun." Let your child interpret his or her art for you, rather than vice versa. (And be ready for some response that may surprise you or tell you something important.)

Feel free to join in with your child. Children benefit from the company of an adult in creative activities if the adult is relaxed and nonjudgmental about the outcome. Just enjoy the *doing*.

21

Drawing Your Grief

Making marks on paper with pens, markers, crayons, or pencil is a powerful experience for a grieving child. To see the results of one's actions demonstrates to the child that he or she has some influence in his or her world. To see his or her hand moving and creating something visible (even if not recognizable) shows the child that he or she is truly alive.

Children also benefit from nonverbal communication and putting their thoughts and feelings on paper in whatever manner they choose. It is important for adults and other children not to direct the grieving child in what or how to create on paper. Provide as rich a variety of materials as possible and let your child direct his or her own efforts. Children may be able to begin to talk about their losses once they have had the chance to express themselves nonverbally.

Creating art to honor and remember someone who has died or moved away or a pet that has died is also a powerful benefit to a child.

Supplies

Paper of any size, but the larger, the better
Crayons, markers, pens, paint and brushes, small sponges
Magazines to cut up
Scissors
Glue stick, tape

Directions

1. Invite your child to draw or paint in any manner he or she wishes. Offer this opportunity often, keeping the pictures.
2. Ask your child if he or she would like to draw pictures about either of the following:
   - What his or her life was like before the loss.
   - What his or her life is like now since the loss.
3. Look at the pictures with your child and discuss what each means. Ask your child what he or she is feeling and thinking, or remembering and wishing.
4. Add the pictures to your child's Memory Book.

Variation

- Tear or cut pictures from magazines and paste them on paper as a collage. Place them in a Memory Book.

22

Touch of Play Dough

Playing with play dough or clay (homemade or purchased) requires the use of hands and fingers and naturally helps in the release of small muscle grief energy. It also helps a child create a concrete and visible symbol of his or her life experiences. While your child plays with clay, he or she is totally in charge of the outcome. During times of grief, there is little a child can control, so this kind of play offers a sense of power. Do not make a model for your child to copy. Let your child make anything he or she wishes. It doesn't need to be recognizable; kneading the clay to release grief energy is the goal.

Recipe for play dough

2 1/2 cups white flour
1/2 cup table salt
2 packages dry unsweetened Kool-Aid
3 tablespoons vegetable oil
2 cups boiling water

1. Mix flour, salt, and Kool-Aid together in large bowl.
2. Mix vegetable oil and boiling water together and pour over dry mix.
3. Stir until ball forms. Knead on flat surface until smooth.

Supplies

Cookie cutters and dull table knives
Rolling pin
Plastic straws cut in short lengths (optional)

Directions

Put the clay on a flat, clean surface and let your child mess around with it. When finished, store in a plastic bag.

Variation

- Make a portable balloon stress ball. Fill a sturdy small balloon with flour by inserting a funnel into the balloon opening. Pour in enough flour to fill the balloon (it is not going to be blown up). Tie the opening of the balloon tightly. Let your child carry this around and squeeze it whenever he or she feels like releasing grief energy from small muscles.

23

Feeling Faces

Paper is a product very adaptable to the needs of grieving children. Manipulating it assists children to release small muscle grief energy when they draw, write, fold, and cut. Your child can create any number of things that have symbolic meaning.

The goals of the games and activities that follow are to help children identify how different feelings show on people's faces and increase children's knowledge of words to describe feelings.

Supplies

Faces copied by machine or hand from pages 114-115
Magazines to cut up (optional)
Index cards
Glue or tape
Pen or pencil, markers
Paper, 8½ x 11 inches

Directions

Make the card deck

1. Copy the illustrations on pages 114 and 115 and paste each face on an index card. Or look through magazines to find pictures of people's faces. Cut them out and paste or tape each one on an index card. Look for at least ten different expressions.
2. Write 20 different feeling words on 20 blank index cards. (See page 115 for some possibilities.)
3. You should have ten face cards and 20 word cards.

Game #1: Matching Feelings

1. Place all feeling face cards face down in a pile. Place all feeling word cards face down in another pile.
2. Player turns over one card from each pile and says whether or not he or she thinks the word card matches the feeling face card. There is no right or wrong answer. Keep turning over a card from each pile until the player finds two cards he or she thinks are a match. (For example, a happy expression and the word joyful.)
3. Help your child expand his or her feeling words vocabulary by suggesting unfamiliar words he or she can use.

Game #2: Say a Feeling

1. Place the feeling face cards face up in a pile.
2. Player names the feeling each card in the pile shows.
3. Repeat with all cards again and use a different word that means the same or nearly the same. For example, mad, angry, and furious might all fit one of the pictures.

Game #3: Share a Story

1. Place the feeling face cards face up in a row, so that you and your child can see each one.
2. Player tells a story from his or her life, or creates a make-believe story. As the story unfolds, pick up the feeling face card that matches the feeling of the child in the story. For example, if the child is telling a story about the first day at a new school, when he felt scared and didn't know if the other kids would like him, he might pick up a face that looks scared or apprehensive or worried. The same feeling face card can be used more than once in a story.
3. Write the story down for your child and add it to the Memory Book (page 85).

Feeling Faces

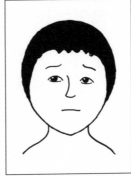
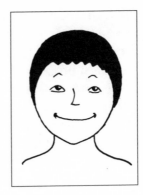

Words for Feelings

Ambivalent
Angry
Annoyed
Brave
Confused
Content
Curious
Depressed
Disappointed
Eager
Embarrassed
Excited
Frustrated
Furious
Happy
Joyful
Mad
Proud
Sad
Satisfied
Scared
Silly
Terrified
Worried

Game #4: *House of Feeling Faces*

1. Begin to make a house with four walls by propping four cards together to form a square, feeling faces showing on the outside of the house. Gently lay cards on top to form the roof (or floor) and then prop another four cards together to form the second story, feelings always face out.
3. As your child builds the house, talk about all the feelings that people have in their homes. Tell your child that all feelings are okay, though hurtful actions are not.

Variations with paper

- Make origami birds and other animals. Look for origami pattern books at the public library.
- Make old-fashioned paper hats and airplanes.
- Draw pictures.
- Make paper dolls and clothes. Color them.

24

Doodling

Doodling is any random drawing of small figures, designs, and scribbles a child may feel like doing. Research shows that doodlers tend to remember what they hear more than non-doodlers. Children who are grieving can release grief energy and increase their learning capacities at the same time. Some kinds of doodles help the right side and the left side of the brain communicate better.

Supplies

Large pieces of paper
Pens and markers
Tape

Directions

1. Fold three pieces of paper in half and crease them. Open them back up and tape each piece to a flat surface where your child can reach the paper to draw on it.

2. Taking a pen or marker in *each* hand (it doesn't matter whether your child is left- or right-handed), doodle on each half of one piece of paper, both hands drawing at the same time. Keep each hand's drawing to its half of the paper. The two hands do not need to doodle the same thing.

3. Moving to a fresh sheet of paper, begin drawing the *same* thing at the same time on both halves of the paper, a pen or marker in each hand again. Tell your child to move his or her head and eyes while drawing.

4. On the third piece of paper, tell your child to draw a lazy 8 with his or her dominant hand only. (A lazy 8 lies on its side like a child's train track.) Follow the movement of the hand with the head. Draw at least three lazy 8's.

5. Switch to the undominant hand and draw more lazy 8's.

6. Hold the pen or marker with *both* hands at once and draw more lazy 8's, head and eyes following the pattern. Repeat as often as the child wishes.

25

Time Ball: Memories on a String

Women of the Yakama Native American Tribe in Washington State documented the stories of their lives many, many years ago by placing beads at intervals on string. When the string got too long for convenience, they wound it up into a ball. It was called a "Time Ball" because each bead marked an important time in its owner's life. Each Time Ball was like a personal journal or calendar. The women would get together and share the stories of their lives by unraveling their Time Balls and recounting each event.

Down through the years people have adapted the concept of the Time Ball to other uses. Grieving children can make their own Time Balls to honor their lives and losses. Share this story with your child and suggest that a Time Ball of his or her life would help to keep memories of a loved one strong.

Supplies

Sturdy string

Beads, buttons, feathers, or other small items that can be attached to the string

Directions

1. Cut a 3-foot length of string.
2. Gather small treasured items or provide a collection of beads and buttons to put on the string.
3. Help your child decide what event to put first and choose a bead or button or treasure to represent it. For example, the child's birth could start the string, or the child's first vivid memory of the person or pet that has died or moved away.
4. Starting at one end of the string, make a knot one inch from the end. Slide the bead or other treasure onto the string up against the knot. Tie another knot so that the bead is between the two knots and can't move. This first bead represents the first event your child wishes to remember and honor.
5. Keep adding beads, etc. to the string, each about an inch or so from the previous one, as your child chooses a new event to add to the string or as new events happen in your child's life. Remember to tie a knot first, then slide on the bead or other item, then tie another knot.
6. Ask your child if he or she would like to talk about what each bead represents. Respect a no.

7. Every now and then as the weeks, months, and years pass, pull out the Time Ball and add beads. Remember that the last item put on the string represents the most recent event because the Time Ball is a chronological record from earliest time (at the beginning of the string) to most recent time.

8. Once you come to the end of the string, cut an additional length of string and tie it firmly to the end of the Time Ball next to the most recent event.

9. Store the Time Ball in a special place where it is safe and can be pulled out to look at and to help your child remember all the events he or she has put on it.

Variation

- Make a Time Ball for yourself as your child makes one. The two of you can share your stories from time to time just as the women of the Yakama Native American Tribe used to do.

Words of Encouragement

As you know, caring for a grieving child can be a big job, one that is certainly difficult to anticipate or prepare for. When loss occurs, many dreams may be shattered, and it can take a long time for a child to accept this and build a life afterward.

The information in this book gives you classic, uncomplicated methods to get through a difficult time. Your goal in supporting a grieving child is to fill the painful void with constructive knowledge and activities—to do something, even when it appears there is nothing to do.

Care givers often worry if they are doing the right thing or the most beneficial thing. You should know that your grieving child will remember in a positive way far into the future any effort to care for and support him or her (especially with the information you now have). Your hope is that your child will be able to live through *all* his or her life experiences and learn skills that enable him or her to build new relationships, while cherishing the memories of those people (or pets) lost.

It can take years for a child to accept a loss, so it may be a long time before you see the benefits for your child of the care and support you offer. Because children show their grief in their behavior—some of which will be difficult to imagine!—your experience in parenting or care giving may be far different from what you dreamed it would be. This difference will be a loss for you, too.

I encourage you to persist and persevere, at your own unique pace, in finding ways to survive and even thrive during this journey of loss and grief. As you go down the path, be sure to honor your own grief process, too.

Blessings to you and your child!

Acknowledgments

Since 1981 my work has given me the opportunity to use the material in this book with children and adults. Whether supporting a kindergartner whose father and mother died within months of one another, assisting a new mother whose baby died at birth, or playing "Beauty Shop" with children living in foster care, I have been graced with extraordinary experiences through the losses suffered by my clients and students. To all of you who allowed me to travel your grief journeys with you, I thank you for teaching me.

To the many individuals and organizations for giving me encouragement and guidance, I extend my appreciation. In particular, I want to acknowledge Connie Dawson and Pam Hopkins, who spent many hours in conversation with me about grief and loss. To Kathy Starr, Vicki Adams, Rosanne and Bruce Bacon, thank you for your unwavering support for my work. Blessings to Donna Rayforth and Carol Schneider for assisting me with the original research that was the seed of this book.

I also wish to honor those who provided expertise, either through professional training or theoretical resources that were adapted to fit this book. These people include Cynthia White of the Dougy Center, National Center for Grieving Children and Families in Portland, Oregon, Carole Gesme, Jon Pederson, Paul and Gail Dennison, Jean Illsley Clarke, Bruce Perry, Barbara Oehlberg, Russell Friedman, James W. John, Carla Hannaford, Earl Hipp, Michael Discuss, Terry Hicks, Richard Eberst, William Worden, Gerald L. Sittser, and Claudia Jewett Jarratt. Thanks also to Shirley Knox, Rand Dressner, and Barbara and Jerry Benjamin of the Annie Tran Center for Grief and Loss in Prosser, Washington and Elaine Childs-Gowell, who read the early draft and lent critical guidance. Thanks also to my writing group for their support.

To Elizabeth Crary and Carolyn Threadgill of Parenting Press—thank you for asking for a book like this and for helping me make it real.

Index

More Good Books from Parenting Press

The Way I Feel provides a means of introducing both the concepts and the vocabulary that help children express their emotions. Vivid and imaginative full-color illustrations and short poems encourage children to understand how they and others feel. Author and illustrator Janan Cain. Ages 3 to 8 years. Cloth, $16.95.

Dealing with Disappointment: Helping Kids Cope When Things Don't Go Their Way helps parents teach children how to handle the dozens of disappointments everyone experiences daily. Covers what to do when kids are upset, teaches calming strategies and problem solving, and shows how adults can stay calm when kids aren't. Author Elizabeth Crary. Ages 2 to 12 years. Paperback, $14.95.

Time-In: When Time-Out Doesn't Work offers new insight into what children desperately need with the adults in their lives: connection and trust. "Time-in" prevents many problems by helping parents teach children how to be competent, to think, and to succeed. Author Jean Illsley Clarke. Ages 1 to 12 years. Paperback, $10.95.